Voices and Choices
in Coursework

Geographical
Association

Photo: Mark Jones

Theory INTO Practice

Voices and Choices in Coursework

**SUSAN MARTIN,
ALAN REID,
KATE BULLOCK
AND KEITH BISHOP**

PROFESSIONAL DEVELOPMENT
FOR GEOGRAPHY TEACHERS
Series editors: Mary Biddulph and Graham Butt

Geographical
Association

Acknowledgments

We would like to thank the schools, students, teachers, teacher researchers and parents who took part in the research. The original study, written by Susan Martin, Kate Bullock, Keith Bishop and Alan Reid at the University of Bath, was financially supported by the ESRC, Research Award No. R000222684.

The Geographical Association would like to thank Mark Jones (Faculty of Education, University of the West of England) for supplying the photographs for this book.

The authors

Susan Martin, Alan Reid, Kate Bullock and Keith Bishop are lecturers in the Department of Education, University of Bath, Claverton Down, Bath BA2 7AY. Contact details: s.martin@bath.ac.uk or a.d.reid@bath.ac.uk.

The series editors

Dr Mary Biddulph is Lecturer in Geography Education in the School of Education, University of Nottingham and Dr Graham Butt is Senior Lecturer in Geographical Education in the School of Education, University of Birmingham.

ISBN 1 84377 058 X
First published 2002
Impression number 10 9 8 7 6 5 4 3 2 1
Year 2005 2004 2003

Published by the Geographical Association, 160 Solly Street, Sheffield S1 4BF
E-mail: ga@geography.org.uk
Website: www.geography.org.uk
The Geographical Association is a registered charity: no 313129.

The Publications Officer of the GA would be happy to hear from other potential authors who have ideas for geography books. You may contact the Officer via the GA at the address above. The views expressed in this publication are those of the authors and do not necessarily represent those of the Geographical Association.

Designed by Ledgard Jepson Limited
Printed in China through Colorcraft Ltd, Hong Kong

Contents

Editors' preface

Theory into Practice is dedicated to improving both teaching and learning in geography. The over-riding element in the series is direct communication with the classroom practitioner about current research in geographical education and how this relates to classroom practice. Geography teachers from across the professional spectrum will be able to access research findings on particular issues which they can then relate to their own particular context.

How to use this series

This series also has a number of other concerns. First, we seek to achieve the further professional development of geography teachers and their departments. Second, each book is intended to support teachers' thinking about key aspects of teaching and learning in geography and encourages them to reconsider these in the light of research findings. Third, we hope to reinvigorate the debate about how to teach geography and to give teachers the support and encouragement to revisit essential questions, such as:

- Why am I teaching this topic?
- Why am I teaching it in this way?
- Is there a more enjoyable/challenging/interesting/successful way to teach this?
- What are the students learning?
- How are they learning?
- Why are they learning?

This list is by no means exhaustive and there are many other key questions which geography teachers can and should ask. However, the ideas discussed and issues raised in this series provide a framework for thinking about practice. Fourth, each book should offer teachers of geography a vehicle within which they can improve the quality of teaching and learning in their subject; and an opportunity to arm themselves with the new understandings about geography and geographical education. With this information teachers can challenge current assumptions about the nature of the subject in schools. The intended outcome is to support geography teachers in becoming part of the teaching and learning debate. Finally, the series aims to make classroom practitioners feel better informed about their own practice through consideration of, and reflection upon, the research into what they do best – teach geography.

Mary Biddulph and Graham Butt
January 2002

Introduction

This book is based on a research project in which the authors worked with geography and English teachers to explore principles and practices for effective student learning through GCSE coursework. The project investigated coursework as a framework for learning and as a context for developing and enhancing the transferable skills that are associated with creativity, critical thinking and independent learning. This book is intended to inform and influence practice in geography teaching by:

- presenting the findings from the project;
- placing these findings in a wider context of current debate about coursework, learning, teaching and assessment; and,
- raising issues and questions for geography teachers to consider in relation to their own practice.

Chapter 1 introduces the assessment and lifelong learning debate, and the framework and context for the project (see Reid and Jones, 2002, for an overview). Chapters 2-5 focus on themes emerging from the research: students as evaluators of their own work (Chapter 2), students' perceptions of marking criteria (Chapter 3), using fieldwork to enhance student learning in coursework (Chapter 4), and the 'rules of engagement' for coursework (Chapter 5). Chapter 6 suggests ways forward for the research and for teachers.

Each chapter discusses examples from the data, general patterns within the findings and broader considerations on the topics, and includes questions designed to prompt further reflection on the emerging themes. Learning, teaching and assessment emerge as interwoven dimensions to school geography and are discussed as such throughout.

Our approach is to encourage teachers to review their own practice in the light of findings grounded in data, rather than identifying what effective geography teaching looks like or working back from 'good practice'. The book is data- rather than theory-led and thus subject to the limitations and strengths one might expect of such an approach. We hope that by 'comparing notes' with the perspectives, opinions and evidence presented, teachers will be encouraged to re-assess appropriate ways of helping students with coursework in their own contexts. It should also ensure that students' coursework meets the examination requirements *and* fulfils more of its potential.

We recognise that improving learning and teaching is every geography teacher's aim, however, it is not always feasible, realistic or easy to put 'theory' into 'practice'. *Voices and Choices in Coursework* should act as a catalyst for geography teachers to reflect on their approaches to teaching in and through coursework. Also, by discussing examples of current classroom and departmental practice it will help teachers to re-evaluate the links between learning and assessment.

Finally, we do not subscribe to McNamara's fallacy – making the measurable important rather than important measurable – we hope this book will encourage and support geography teachers in straddling the inevitable tensions between assessment *of* learning and assessment *for* learning.

Photo: Mark Jones.

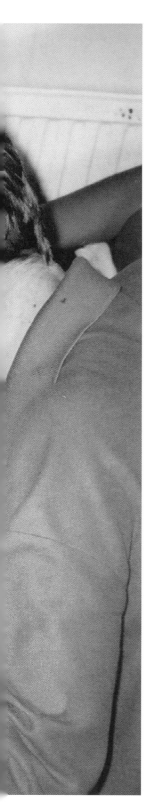

1: Learning through GCSE coursework

Coursework is a major part of all geography courses for the General Certificate of Secondary Education (GCSE). The marks awarded and the geographical skills applied contribute to the particular significance of coursework in geography for students and teachers alike. This book is based on a study funded by the Economic and Social Research Council (ESRC), which was carried out as a collaborative inquiry between a team of university and teacher researchers. The team worked in six case-study schools in the South-West of England. Data were collected from geography and English teachers through interviews and discussion about how their coursework practices contributed to student learning.

Background to the study

The broad aim of the research was to explore the potential of GCSE coursework as a framework for learning. Within this aim, specific objectives were to investigate:

- the extent to which the original qualities attributed to coursework are achieved in current practice;

- the extent to which coursework contributes to the development of skills associated with independent learning, critical thinking and creativity;

- the influence of the demands of assessment upon students' learning.

The departments in the six case-study schools represent a range of school population sizes, socio-economic contexts and funding arrangements. The teachers selected individual students for interview to ensure a balance across gender and levels of attainment within and across the schools. For further information about the study please visit the ESRC research database (at www.regard.ac.uk), and a summary of the main findings is presented in Reid and Jones, 2002.

Findings have emerged from the study which we believe will contribute towards restoring a more authentic form of assessment by challenging some of the current underlying, and undermining, issues associated with public examinations, in particular GCSEs. As an element of the first public examination for students it seems to us ironic that coursework should embrace, simultaneously, principles of authentic assessment and requirements that militate against these (as a result of the accepted norms and rigours of a public assessment system). We recognise the difficulty that schools face in the current drive for accountability, but note the strong concerns of teachers taking part in the study that coursework should not fall foul of the clamour of demands for accountability or fair (in the sense of reliable) assessment systems.

The assessment debate and lifelong learning

At the inception of the GCSE, coursework was regarded as a central component of the examination. It was envisaged that coursework would raise the validity of the assessment process and enhance the learning of students by providing a useful vehicle for communication skills and giving students credit for initiating tasks and assuming responsibility for their own work (SEC, 1985). Almost 15 years later the focus of the examination has shifted towards the use of GCSE outcomes as a measure of school performance and accountability with the result that both the reliability and the value of the coursework component have been brought into question (Tattersall, 1994). This is despite two recent contributions to the debate about coursework and learning, namely the Green Paper, *The Learning Age* (DfEE, 1998), and the report of the National Advisory Committee on Creative and Cultural Education (NACCCE) (DfEE, 1999). They argue that schools – through classwork, homework and coursework – should provide opportunities for students to acquire knowledge and skills associated with creativity, critical thinking and independent learning in an attempt to foster and sustain lifelong learning.

Significantly, in recent years (see, for example, Black and Wiliam, 1998; Foskett, 2000), greater emphasis has been given to the formative role of assessment in terms of:

- raising awareness as to this function of assessment;

- related benefits regarding students' learning and achievement; and

- the need to address it specifically – while there is opportunity to use formative assessment in the classroom, by default, it tends to go unnoticed and unaddressed.

Coursework – the teacher assessed component of study which Gipps (1992) argues is the least constrained form of authentic or performance assessment – is an obvious element which retains the potential to encourage the development of creativity, critical thinking and the capacity for lifelong learning. Paradoxically, the very skills that are now being squeezed out are those that, from its conception, GCSE coursework was designed to encourage.

The principles for developing skills associated with independent learning and critical thinking relate also to other aspects of teaching geography. Homework, like coursework, for instance, will not fulfil its potential if it does not include opportunities for students to develop these skills and, perhaps more importantly, if the relevant criteria for their identification and assessment are not made explicit (Balderstone and Lambert, 1999).

Similarly, fieldwork presents opportunities to develop thinking skills, but the expectation that by doing fieldwork thinking skills are automatically developed is unhelpful. Foskett (2000) argues that while fieldwork presents appropriate opportunities, students and teachers must be both aware of these and of how they can be developed. Unfortunately, formative assessment is often not pursued in fieldwork because teachers perceive that it requires an (additional) investment of their time. Yet ensuring students understand their coursework focus and the assessment criteria is significant in maximising their attainment (Black and Wiliam, 1998; Howes and Flinders, 1998), because it makes it easier for the teacher to mark and offer formative feedback. A rejoinder here is that guidelines for students, while necessary, are not sufficient in themselves, as we will show in Chapter 2.

The formative potential of the process of completing coursework suggests that risk-taking can sit more comfortably within such a process. Thus, for example, low-stakes assessment can be high risk. However, at GCSE the summative dimension to the assessment of coursework makes it high stakes and militates against the very nature of a low-stakes assessment process. We think it is incumbent to consider the extent to which skills and strategies associated with risk-taking can become more integrated into formative assessment. In so doing, formative assessment then becomes a feature of all work and has less of a high risk nature, thereby supporting and enabling students' creativity, critical thinking and independent learning.

Points to consider

- What are the key issues and considerations in your school for supporting student learning through coursework?

- What are your priorities in assessment?

- How do you respond to the debate about lifelong learning?

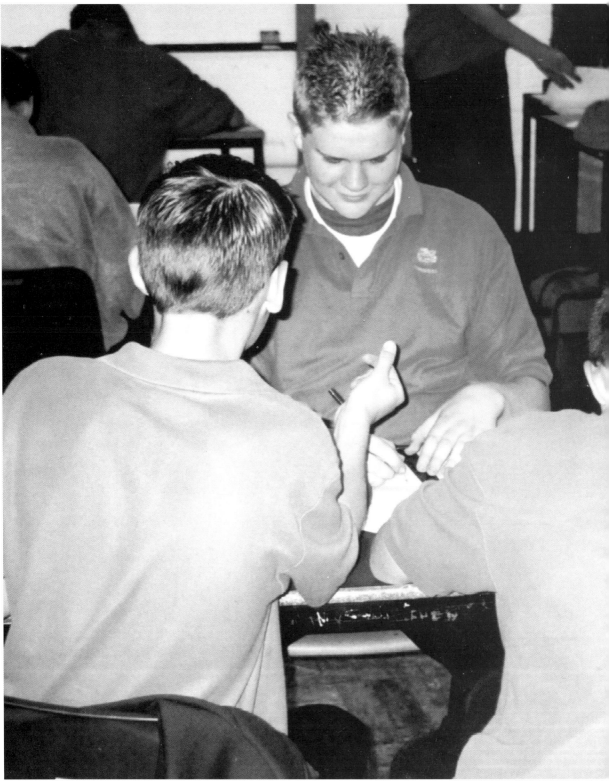

Photo: Mark Jones.

2: Students as evaluators

Teacher: *[The students] can be led to achieve reasonable standards in describing their data, but when it comes to analysing it and giving evaluations of it, then it becomes far more difficult ... It's the evaluation where they need most help ... we say to them 'Have you found evidence to support or reject that hypothesis? Has your information confirmed what you expected?' ... I like to put them in the position of being in court and saying 'Have you proved or disproved this particular theory?' and think of it in those terms.*

Students are used to having their work assessed and judged by their teachers. They see it as a means of identifying what they have attained and use it to compare their own outcomes with their peers. Students are less used to assessing and judging their own work and identifying strengths and weaknesses. Self-assessment is a form of critical evaluation that involves gathering evidence in order to make judgements about the quality of your own work or actions such that you can make improvements, i.e. it has a formative dimension. For learning to be effective, students need to be able to recognise quality, compare generic standards to their own work and be able to rationalise and articulate that knowledge and understanding. In this chapter, we discuss data on students' understanding of evaluation, the match between students' and teachers' perceptions, strategies for enhancing students' evaluation skills, and evaluating learning in fieldwork.

Students' understanding of evaluation

Although in its original conception coursework was intended to enhance the autonomy and capability of students in all aspects of learning, our study indicates that many teachers feel that the development of techniques or skills of critical evaluation is often too complex for some GCSE students. Interviews with students showed that, in general, their understanding of critical thinking and evaluation was limited and unsophisticated. They focused on criticism (often negative), being critical and being sceptical (see Bailin, 1999). Students had difficulty in shifting from believing that questioning and evaluation were something that was done *to* them rather than something that should be done *by* them.

We found that students, working at the whole-class or individual level, associated critical thinking with high stress situations. Teacher-student interactions designed to monitor the production of coursework were often viewed as situations where the 'cards are stacked' in the teacher's favour and can be perceived by students as confrontations and challenges to their individuality and identity. In contrast, all groups valued student-student interactions in small group work (e.g. discussing texts and media in English, carrying out fieldwork in geography) as more conducive to fostering skills of critical thinking and reflection (Morehouse, 1997).

The match between students' and teachers' perceptions

In general, teachers conceived of critical thinking in terms of logic, explanation, rationality and controversy – in particular, political and ideological contestation. In terms of coursework skills, in the execution of their GCSE coursework students did not readily realise these conceptions. Although teachers worked to encourage critical and evaluative skills such as questioning prior knowledge and experience, testing out and applying new knowledge, and promoting learner responsibility through reflection and evaluation, even some capable students failed to associate these skills with success in coursework. Teachers believed that these are difficult skills for GCSE students. Only in a few higher attaining students was perception of relevance to other tasks and subjects realised and pursued.

In respect of working towards and identifying good coursework, despite teachers' concern that coursework should, for example, demonstrate a coherent argument, students invariably believed content and presentation to be most important in meeting the assessment criteria. Although some students acknowledged that critical and creative learning (indicated by structure, argument and understanding) would 'get them marks', only a few knew how and why they should show it in their coursework. Students tended to equate more effort with more writing and hence the achievement of higher grades; their view was that 'more equals better'. When asked how they might have improved their coursework, students' responses indicated that they would have included more detail, have spent more time on it and have presented it better in terms of spelling and grammar.

Strategies for enhancing evaluation skills

Geography teachers agreed that the evaluation requirement of a coursework project demands engagement with critical thinking processes; they also acknowledged the difficulties in preparing their students effectively for this. Some schools provided their students with highly structured templates of how an evaluation should be written. Others felt that enabling strategies, such as discussions and explanations of the nature and processes of critical evaluation, allowed those students (who had not previously understood that there might be more than one way to undertake an enquiry) to develop critical skills more fully. For lower attaining students, a lack of observable critical and evaluative skills was also deemed to be contingent on a more fundamental difficulty in describing investigations and expressing their findings in writing as the comment below indicates.

> **Teacher:** *They can explain things [verbally], but as soon as it comes to putting it down on paper and having to record it in that way, they struggle and don't have some of the techniques needed – the grammar, especially.*

In terms of coursework practice, 'thinking through geography' strategies (Leat, 1998) and field-based investigations into controversial issues were highlighted as facilitating structured questioning strategies which develop critical thinking skills:

> **Teacher:** *I might give them several suggestions and pull several suggestions out of them – 'How might you go about doing this?' and then write the suggestions down. So it might be ways in which they can present work, things they can do with data. They have particular problems with conclusions and evaluations and they also have problems – they can pick out that field number one had the most litter in it, but quite often they find it difficult to see that it's because field number one was next to the car park. So it's trying to prompt those things out of them. It's those elements that get them the highest marks.*

In addition to the courtroom tactics described above, teachers suggested another strategy to encourage students to question ideas and approaches, and to offer well-argued alternatives:

> **Teacher:** *I always like to set the question 'If you had unlimited time and resources how would you do things differently?' I think a lot of very interesting ideas come out and the students can reflect upon problems they may have had in the field and think carefully how could those problems have been solved.*

One teacher felt strongly that holding a whole-class discussion, which allowed relevant arguments and theories to be shared, was beneficial for all. Several teachers agreed that this is a particularly powerful tactic with mixed ability groups and some also stressed the value of mixing abilities for small-group work.

> **Teacher:** *Mixed ability teaching does help with that. If we were setted, bottom set students would never see the creative ideas that the B and A and A* students were coming out with. By teaching mixed ability you open everyone up to those ideas. Also remembering that some D/E candidates are superb orally. They'll come out with the fantastic ideas, which perhaps no one else does.*

Help in capturing ideas and structuring thinking was also used by a number of teachers to ensure that evidence for reflection was not lost because some students were disinclined to record their findings or discussions in writing.

Teacher: *What I then tend to do is talk it through with them and write down for them any points we've raised and discussed. So they may come up with the answer, but I act as a scribe in fact and write those ideas down for them so that they've got a log and a record, because after a conversation they forget. I also think as staff we sometimes forget they're not just doing our subject, they're doing many others.*

Points to consider

• Are the strategies for encouraging evaluation and critical thinking suggested above sufficient?

• Do they match your own approaches?

• How can you further develop your students' skills of evaluation and critical thinking?

Evaluating the learning in fieldwork

Many of the students' perceptions of coursework differed from their teachers in relation to the evaluation of their fieldwork. Students displayed little awareness of their expected and actual attainment through fieldwork, attributing the greatest status to:

• their performance on the day of the fieldwork *rather than* before or afterwards;

• composing and presenting the fieldwork *rather than* planning and evaluating their investigations; and

• summative comments of the teacher on the completion of the piece of work *rather than* to any formative comments from teachers, their peers or themselves.

Only a few of the highest attaining students reported and illustrated either a sense of their own progression in the subject or a sense of development in their performance as geography students through their GCSE fieldwork.

The wider educational research literature links student understandings of themselves as learners in terms of progression and development to priorities for critical thinking, active engagement and reflection for student learning– particularly through the use of self- and peer-assessment tasks. Black and Wiliam's review of research on teacher assessment stresses that these features are crucial to the educational progress of students as they become able 'to picture their own learning in the light of what it means to get better' (1998, p. 30). We note that the discussion of assessment in geographical education often omits reference to the significance and role of using formative assessment in:

• developing good practice in student fieldwork;

• supporting and enhancing student learning; and

• maximising GCSE candidate performance

(Howes and Flinders, 1998; Butt, 2000; Lambert, 2000).

Strategies that teachers and learners might use for formative assessment during coursework include:

- sharing learning intentions with students;

- sharing assessment objectives and criteria with students;

- sharing examples of good student practice with other students; and

- encouraging students to reflect on their progress. (Howes and Hopkin, 2000).

The next chapter illustrates these strategies further by discussing students' perceptions of the marking criteria, the importance of sharing marking criteria with students effectively, students' interpretations of teachers' messages, and developing criticality and independent learning.

Points to consider

We have stated that 'for learning to be effective, students need to be able to recognise quality, compare generic standards to their own work and be able to rationalise and articulate that knowledge and understanding.'

- What is your response to this statement?

- Do you provide your students with opportunities to do this?

- What might be the key issues for your department to explore?

The acknowledged and unresolved tension perplexing most teachers is the pull between providing structured coursework with strong student guidance in pursuit of a valuable additional mark or two, and offering less constrained support in order to develop students' independent learning about geographical enquiry, together with their skills of evaluation and critical thinking.

- What is your own view on this 'support/independent learning' dilemma?

- To what extent would you expect colleagues to share the same view?

Photo: Mark Jones.

3: Getting high marks

> **Researcher:** *So tell me what you have to do to get high marks.*
>
> **Student:** *Write more writing. Like, if you spread it out you get more [marks], and make sure you have full stops and things like that.*

Sharing marking criteria with students

Research evidence suggests that sharing marking criteria with students is effective practice (Black and Wiliam, 1998). It would seem self-evident that identifying the goals for the students to aim at is what most teachers would do. However, the messages that teachers give are not necessarily the ones received by the students. Our research suggests that students get very different ideas about the targets they are aiming for, while teachers believe that they have been clear in communicating their messages to the students. In this chapter we focus on students' perceptions of marking criteria and provide examples to illustrate the issues and tensions this may create when they do not coincide with the teacher's.

Clearly evident in our study was the teachers' awareness of the importance of sharing the marking scheme (or criteria) with the students. Equally, many students were aware that marking schemes existed and needed to be taken into consideration. Nevertheless, some students seemed to be under the impression they were not allowed to know what the marking criteria were, though teachers clearly considered they were translating the criteria to make them more accessible to the students. The gap seems to lie in the students' and teachers' different interpretations.

Hitting the 'buttons'

Students interpreted teacher's messages in different ways. Lower attainers latched on to different messages given by teachers without applying any obvious sense of discrimination about the relative importance or significance of the message. The extract from one interview indicates how students repeatedly cited presentational factors as being what their geography teacher was looking for:

> **Researcher:** *Do you know how to do well with coursework?*
>
> **Student:** *Well, planning is where you write everything down, because if you go straight into it you could do it wrong.*
>
> **Researcher:** *Could you tell me what you have to do to get high marks?*
>
> **Student:** *More paragraphs ... speech marks, all the grammar things and the style and the way you write it.*

Even when one might think this student is on the right track, e.g. by suggesting that careful planning is important, responses about getting good marks were often determined by factors related to how the coursework looks rather than what it conveys about her knowledge and understanding.

At a higher level, students applied learned 'rules of thumb' and would recite them almost as a mantra. Clearly teachers had spelt out the messages, but the students were finding it difficult to interpret them.

> **Researcher:** *What would earn high marks in your opinion?*
>
> **Student:** *Good use of language, like graphic about lots of detail, little things that you have to go into detail about.*
>
> **Researcher:** *When you say graphic, do you mean being descriptive?*
>
> **Student:** *Yes.*
>
> **Researcher:** *Is there any guidance given to you as to what makes a good piece of coursework?*
>
> **Student:** *Yes, we get the sheets that show you how to use descriptive language ...*
>
> **Researcher:** *So if it is descriptive, and is written well, will that earn high marks?*
>
> **Student:** *Yes, that is as far as you know, before you hand it in.*

In this instance, the student's interpretation of the messages he is receiving imposes a ceiling on his attainment. Unless the teacher picks up on his focus on description, his access to higher marks is limited.

Perhaps more worryingly was the students' preoccupation with quantity, for example believing that better marks would accrue from doing 'more of the same', working harder, writing more detail, but with little recognition that a critical focus on what they were doing is essential. Other students, however, grasped the idea that they need to 'hit' those 'buttons' their teachers have indicated 'get them marks' as this extract indicates.

> **Researcher:** *What do you have to do to get high marks?*
>
> **Student:** *In geography, probably do all the little things as well. We do scatter graphs as well, which is what my teacher suggested, and that will help get good marks.*
>
> **Researcher:** *So you know you get good marks in geography if you put in graphs.*
>
> **Student:** *Yes. And drawing up tables.*

A recurring theme in the student responses is the feeling that they have no critical awareness of what they are being asked to do. Students are applying a mechanism for which, almost in a Pavlovian sense, they are expecting a reward. This is apparent in another student's response:

> **Student:** *I did find the geography easy and I got full marks. I think I could have included more, but there wasn't any need to.*
>
> **Researcher:** *What sorts of things would those have been?*
>
> **Student:** *Well I didn't really write a conclusion about the piece and I could have included more graphs and used more bar charts and stuff to show the results, but I just didn't need to, to get the full marks. I don't remember the conclusion bit really well, but we had to write a conclusion on it, and if I remember, I don't think I wrote a particular amount or put any depth into it. Just a summary of what we'd done and then what we'd found out.*

Some students are aware of the messages teachers give about what they need to include in their coursework, but it is obvious that they cannot assess the value or worth of the various components. This student had sensed the need to have a conclusion (he had been told he needed a summary), but there was no indication that he recognised the function a conclusion served beyond the need to have a section that finished the piece of work. In his view, he had 'hit the button'.

Developing criticality

Crudely, we might divide students into two groups in relation to their ability to work with the marking criteria that are used to assess geography coursework. The first group comprises those who are limited or constrained by the framework derived from the criteria. They have engaged to a point where the framework can help them identify what is required (it tells them what the 'buttons' are), but they are not able to see beyond it, nor can they use it as a basis for decision making. The second group, probably much fewer in number, can peer over the edge and identify the opportunities the marking framework offers.

The difference between the two groups lies in their self-awareness of their learning. Put bluntly, students in the first group are not able to assess themselves. If they are able to make sense of the marking criteria their decision making remains constrained by it. They cannot interpret it, nor can they exercise judgement about how they might use it. In contrast, the second group are much more likely to be self-aware. The point of demarcation distinguishing the two groups is that the students in the second group have sufficient critical faculties to be able to interpret the meaning of the framework and its implications and thus derive strategies or approaches to engage in self-improvement. These are the true independent learners who can make rational decisions about how and where best to apply their efforts in order to achieve the greatest reward. They also operate from a different locus of control (see Chapter 5).

At these higher levels, students are clearly able to make sense of what it means to engage with the marking criteria. For example, this student, when asked why other students might get lower marks, demonstrated a degree of insight seen in few of the others:

Researcher: *What did other people do to get lower marks?*

Student: *I think they didn't spend enough time on it or didn't cover the points. They didn't have a good geographical understanding I suppose. It says in the marking criteria that for level 3 you have to be able to use originality and initiative and have a well organised plan and things like that. So people obviously didn't have the skills to apply that.*

Researcher: *Where did you pick up the skills for you to get these things?*

Student: *Well when they said originality and initiative I said to myself 'Obviously I've got to show that' so I went out of my way to do something different to what other people had done, so I asked them what they were doing and tried to do something different. In a sense I wouldn't tell anyone my initiative bit because I didn't want anyone nicking it. So some bits, if I didn't have the mark scheme before, it would obviously be very difficult to grab.*

Researcher: *So having the mark scheme actually helps getting the marks.*

Student: *Yes.*

Towards independent learning

Black and Wiliam (1998) maintain that students can only assess themselves when they have a sufficiently clear picture of the targets that their learning is meant to attain. The implication for teachers is that they need to identify their learners' understanding of the goals that are being set for them. The fact is that such a discussion stage is often missed as teachers and students encounter a perception gap. A key recommendation in Black and Wiliam's work is that unless there are opportunities for students to express their understanding through discussion, then improvements in their learning will be less likely. Such formative processes might seem obvious, but do the questions teachers ask lead to common understandings between themselves and students? Black and Wiliam ask 'Do I really know enough about the understanding of my students to be able to help each of them?' (1998, p. 13). In the next chapter we continue this discussion by exploring the role of fieldwork in enhancing student learning.

Points to consider

- Telling students about the marking criteria is clearly not enough. Knowing what the problem is, is the key to providing the appropriate formative feedback.

- What are your students' conceptions of the learning goals in coursework and what are the implications for teachers?

Photo: Mark Jones.

4: Using fieldwork to enhance student learning

4

> **Student:** *Coursework's better when you find it fun or you enjoy doing it. You seem to get better marks for it, but not always ... I think I quite liked this [piece of coursework] a lot because we could actually go out there and find the data ourselves, whereas in English you have to look at a book and it's a book topic really.*
>
> **Researcher:** *But if the geography piece had been a book one it might have been the same?*
>
> **Student:** *Yes, it might have been a bit more boring.*
>
> **Researcher:** *So the field trip and that kind of thing ...*
>
> **Student:** *Yes, that livened it up a bit.*

The compulsory fieldwork element of GCSE Geography is placed within the broader context of the range of technical and investigative skills deemed essential to geographical study and enquiry by the subject criteria. These skills include:

- identifying geographical questions and issues and establishing appropriate sequences of investigation;

- identifying and collecting evidence from primary [i.e. fieldwork-based], secondary and ICT-based sources, and recording and presenting it;

- describing, analysing and interpreting evidence, making decisions, drawing and justifying conclusions and communicating findings in ways appropriate to the tasks and audience; and

- evaluating the methods of collecting, presenting and analysing evidence, as well as the validity and limitations of evidence and conclusions.

(QCA, 2001, p. 2)

While the research base for the educational value of field enquiry is not as well-developed as that for environmental learning in a broader sense (Rickinson, 2001), evidence documented by Ofsted suggests that high achievement in geography in schools is linked to a high profile for fieldwork in the curriculum (Smith,1997; see also Foskett, 2000). Our own study reveals a number of tensions *between* the expectations, features and purposes that teachers and students ascribe to fieldwork, and *within* the students' experience of organising, recording and explaining the learning that takes place through fieldwork. In this chapter we discuss student and teacher experiences and perspectives on fieldwork in coursework to explore these tensions. We also consider how a greater emphasis on the formative assessment of learning through fieldwork may support and improve student learning through GCSE Geography.

Valuing fieldwork

Unlike most coursework in GCSE subjects, geography fieldwork involves students engaging in a series of learning activities that are grounded in perceptions, experiences and evidence derived from an out-of-school setting (Nowicki, 1999). The educational value of fieldwork has often been linked to the opportunities it presents for cognitive development, alongside affective, social and personal development, and the development of a sense of place. Barratt *et al.* (1997) propose that effective practice in fieldwork in GCSE Geography involves making the experiential learning associated with it both meaningful and purposeful for and by the students themselves, particularly through teachers ensuring that there is progression in student enquiries across key stages 3 and 4. We identify two initial considerations for teacher reflection about learning through fieldwork:

1   Do students and teachers share common understandings of the purposes and opportunities of fieldwork in GCSE Geography?

2   How is a shared understanding communicated, supported and maintained within the frameworks, guidance and events that lead to the submission of GCSE Geography coursework?

Support and structure in fieldwork

An exploration of the considerations outlined above might start by considering the high degrees of *support* and *structuring* that had come to dominate the completion of coursework in the schools in this study (see also Howes and Flinders, 1998). In this research this was typified by a widespread reliance on teacher-prepared worksheets and booklets by students of all abilities in completing their GCSE Geography investigations:

Student 1: *You had tasks to do and boxes to fill in. Things like that.*

Student 2: *We went on a field trip and we were taking notes. We had a sheet to fill, which gave us guidelines to answer questions. We've just had that marked and the teacher has marked it as a GCSE. So we knew where we stood. It was a dummy run.*

Independent learning may include devising and using questionnaires during fieldwork.
Photo: Mark Jones.

In this situation, the student – whether undertaking an 'individual study' independently of other students or writing up a class-wide or group-wide field investigation – is coached explicitly in what to include in his/her coursework, how to include it, and when to ensure the work is completed. As a strategy for securing uniformity, manageability and completion in coursework, this has obvious merits for both students and teachers. However, it is also clear from our research that extensive coaching in coursework militates against independent learning in terms of autonomy, initiative and student-centred learning. More concretely, it restricts the possible levels at which generic learning objectives like key skills might be developed, assessed and accredited (e.g. Nowicki, 1999). If, for example, we consider the key skills framework and Level 2 for Application of Number, students must decide how to collect data or be able to design data collection procedures. Students designing fieldwork or research programmes (accredited at Level 3) is good preparation for AS/A-level key skills accreditation, and, of course, for meeting the subject criteria for GCSE Geography and awards of the higher grades (QCA, 2001).

Our data indicates that developing creativity, critical thinking and independent learning through fieldwork was affected significantly by the degree of coaching from teachers. While some students saw teacher-prepared fieldwork worksheets as a facilitating framework for the coursework, the majority considered their support booklets to be a tightly designed set of rules that they should follow in order to complete it. Deviation from these 'rules', students felt, was both risky and unnecessary if they wanted to achieve the grade that was expected of them (see quote on page 26) – another instance in this study of the artificial 'ceiling' on achievement that guidance, 'tier setting' and expectations can have (see also Chapters 3 and 5).

Understanding student learning through fieldwork

Howes and Flinders observe:

> 'Interestingly, coursework assessment takes no note of the tier of entry. It is a common component for all candidates and as such is assessed against a common set of criteria. This has some implications when advising students about the type of coursework they might undertake. If your cohort of GCSE students includes a wide range of abilities, adopting a "single approach" to setting up coursework may be inappropriate' (1998, p. 204).

Some of the higher attaining students could explain the significance to their learning that the booklet-based approaches to fieldwork tended to encourage within the climate of routinised task completion:

Researcher: *Tell me what you're doing for ... geography.*

Student: *We've just handed in our last geography piece. The title question was 'Do human or physical effects have most impact on the landscape of Lulworth Cove?' and it involved us going out on a fieldtrip. We had to take photos of coastal features, make field sketches, take notes, the teacher was talking us through everything and we had to write down what he was saying and then put it in our own words in the coursework. We had to tackle a question which involved having an introduction, whereby we introduced Lulworth Cove before we went. We found out all we could before we went and then a method section, how we were going to find out everything, a result section about everything we did find out and then we drew a conclusion and evaluation, evaluating how well we did and seeing whether we can make any further conclusions from what we found out. It was very much like a science project.*

On the whole, though, we found that teachers' expectations that students would select and make effective use of fieldwork skills and techniques to support their geographical investigations, and that students would pose questions for investigation, simply did not correspond with the students' accounts of their work. Hence our earlier point about the importance of continuing dialogue for effective learning in coursework, and teachers not simply 'telling students' and 'leaving them to get on with it' (see Chapter 3).

Students suggested that their independence, creativity and critical thinking were largely expressed in how they presented information and where they were given opportunities to develop arguments and ideas. Again though, we found little evidence that teacher support (e.g. through writing frames) was provided for the development of the higher order skills associated with these aspects of learning in geography, beyond the use of task completion worksheets and review sheets for the lower order aspects of these skills. Further, we found that many students simply did not share their teachers' understanding of the purposes of fieldwork, and of how a student's performance and achievements in fieldwork might affect their GCSE grade. Only a minority of students across all the schools commented that the fieldwork component of GCSE Geography coursework was more than simply developing and assessing geographical knowledge, understanding and skills.

Fieldwork – for geography or for learning?

The students' recall about the geographical aspects of their fieldwork was often much more highly detailed and structured than their accounts of other dimensions to learning in their coursework. The planning of the site visit, the application and reworking of concepts, data and themes from their GCSE studies, the testing of hypotheses by empirical methods, and, in some cases, a recognition of the requirement to evaluate their experiences and actions as key aspects of geographical enquiry, demonstrated a high degree of correlation and exchange between the teacher's understanding of this dimension of the students' school geography and that developing in the students. Fieldwork, it seemed, could become a space within the GCSE where teachers and students used the same vocabulary, raised similar and appropriate geographical questions, and got to work on 'real geography' together, based on a common framework of purposes and outcomes.

Interestingly though, unless prompted the students tended to omit reference to the formative aspects of 'feedback' and 'feedforward' regarding their learning in the fieldwork component of their coursework. This was captured quite neatly in the expectation that, once students had been on a field visit, all they were required to do was 'write it up' – a phrase that deserves to be unpacked by geography teachers at length. While students could replay explanations from their fieldwork, critical judgements about the adequacy and development of their own or teacher explanations of geographical matters suggested the (all too) limited scope to which the coursework was being put. The interview data below indicate that, in terms of developing students' capacities regarding learning how to learn (and including dimensions associated with creativity, critical thinking and independent learning), this is especially true.

> **Researcher:** *Tell me about your ... geography coursework.*
>
> **Student:** *In geography we went on a field trip and we had to do the worksheets and then when we got back we just answered some questions for it and then we did little diagrams and said how we collected the data, data presentation, data analysis and then we had to find a conclusion. We did little graphs to show the information.*
>
> **Researcher:** *Did you write it up back here?*
>
> **Student:** *Yes. We just did the sheets at the field trip and a couple of the graphs at night and we did the questions at school.*
>
> **Researcher:** *You do this during your classwork and is it also part of your homework?*
>
> **Student:** *Not at the moment, but it will for the six weeks or so in year eleven.*
>
> **Researcher:** *So sometimes you have to do an evaluation as well?*
>
> **Student:** *We haven't got that far yet, so I don't know if we have to or not.*
>
> **Researcher:** *But you might have to.*
>
> **Student:** *They haven't said anything about it at the moment.*
>
> **Researcher:** *But do you know what you'd have to do?*
>
> **Student:** *Not at the moment, but they'd probably explain it first and we'd write little notes.*

Interviews with parents about their child's coursework suggested a broader conceptual framework than the child's. Here, a lack of parent-child interaction might be regarded as a missed opportunity for parental involvement in helping the student evaluate and complete coursework. Thus, on the whole, the parents too could recall the broad details of the fieldwork (they knew when and where the student went), and they liked to discuss the places their child had visited. But what they also expected the field trip to do was involve their child in collecting 'data and then to think about it and analyse it'.

By way of contrast, for some of the parents' expectations of fieldwork (perhaps indicative of their own experiences of school geography?), were little more than that of a guided tour, with work being set for their children to do. These parents showed little expectation of a requirement to think about or evaluate the experience or any evidence gathered during fieldwork. Where this view was echoed in the student interviews, it tended to be found among the lower attaining groups. These students referred to their experience of coursework primarily in terms of descriptive tasks, and gathering and checking information, rather than being able to identify further purposes of fieldwork and data collection, as in understanding the role of interpretation and evaluating field and enquiry methods. As such, the cognitive and affective gains and the 'accelerated learning' expected of fieldwork by Foskett (2000) within geography coursework often appeared to be little more than patchy in their distribution and actuality in the schools in this study.

Students, parents and teachers all appear to have different expectations of the requirement to evaluate fieldwork experiences on return from visits. Photo: Mark Jones.

Points to consider

In relation to the fieldwork component of GCSE Geography coursework:

- How does your department explain and agree good practice in students' fieldwork and its benefits to student learning?

- How is this communicated with students?

- How do students interpret it?

- What issues are raised by your reflections for your department, coursework guidance and students?

Photo: Mark Jones.

5: Coursework: rules of engagement?

Teacher: *The more structured it is, the less creativity they can normally show, because the more structured you make it, they can't go off on tangents so much. You're constraining them ... But if they are creative they can go off on a complete wobbler and not answer what you want them to.*

Some teachers and departments approach coursework from their own perspective making deliberate choices about structuring, scaffolding and the scope in the interests of maximising students' achievements. This chapter looks specifically at the data that indicated that such tensions existed in the specific area of the locus of control, i.e. the extent to which students were, and realised they were, in charge of their own coursework. It also discusses teachers' influence on the *locus of control*, both explicit and implicit, together with questions and implications that arise from them.

The research indicated that students enjoyed various aspects of coursework, such as experiencing a degree of ownership of their work, and teachers appreciated the relative freedom to work outside the narrow constraints of examination-focused work. However, it was clear that reconciling working towards maximum grades for students in the context of encouraging other skills, such as critical thinking and independent learning, created both a tension and a limitation.

Locus of control

In this study, the locus of control for completing coursework lies largely with teachers, with the exception of higher ability students ('ability' bands identified by the teachers):

- higher ability students typically achieve their potential but some are constrained by the criteria;

- middle ability students can achieve their potential, if they are able to build on the frameworks provided; and

- lower ability students do not achieve their potential, but achieve more than they would without the support they receive.

The following student very definitely saw herself as being in charge of her coursework:

> **Researcher:** *Do you think doing coursework is quite different from the rest of your work?*
>
> **Student:** *Yes, I love coursework because it really gives me a chance to show how good I am at whatever subject because in class it's 'Read this, answer the question, do the comprehension exercise, draw a graph', but it's not a whole project you've put your heart and soul into and completed yourself. And afterwards you get a great sense of satisfaction once you've done a complete piece of coursework and handed it in, whereas in class it's just ongoing. It's very individual when you do your coursework. You do it by yourself and it depends what you think. It's not what someone else thinks. I'm not worried about that. It doesn't bother me that I haven't got the same answer as someone else, because I always try and justify what I've got and I think sometimes that I can get better marks as well because I haven't gone through the same steps as everyone else. I've used something that I've found out myself.*

Here is evidence of the independent learner who is able to make judgements about the value of her own work. She recognises the need and has the ability to justify her actions and writing, which is a key characteristic of a learner who is in control of her learning. In this instance the student is not constrained by the criteria, but embraces them and looks to see how they can be made to work for her.

Interestingly, however, the notion of control was not synonymous with ownership, particularly in respect of fieldwork. Despite the fact that it is teachers who tend to plan and structure much of the fieldwork, students' views were that they owned it as their work. These students viewed fieldwork as qualitatively different from their usual experience of learning in geography. They claimed that the process and product of fieldwork is much more theirs than the teacher's (as with coursework in general), even where it is the teacher who initiates, structures, guides, monitors and reviews much of the planning and completion of the fieldwork component.

Some students went on to explain to the researchers the ways in which fieldwork, to them, is essentially 'geography in practice'. It is a key feature and highlight of their geography GCSE, and the memorable episodes associated with actually being able to go on a field trip (e.g. being allowed out of school, interviewing the public, getting wet in a river study) (see Mackenzie and White, 1982) are what many students most liked to *remember* – 'In geography we're allowed to go out on field studies', and what teachers want their students to remember – 'It's so much more important, it's going to stay with them a lot longer'. Thus, the notion of geography in practice promoted a real sense of ownership for students, albeit with or without a sense of control.

Structuring students' work

Teachers generally think that making choices for students is necessary, for example, for the purposes of differentiation. In the case of lower attaining geography students there was a consensus that structuring was necessary to maximise marks attained. This was particularly so that students would not miss aspects of the assessment criteria, despite Howes and Flinders' (1998) observations about tier of entry and single approaches to coursework (see page 28).

Teachers had developed different strategies to help lower attaining students gain the highest possible marks in coursework. For example, some teachers were careful in their choice of work, while others saw this selection as less significant than the choice of approach for the task (surveying traffic, interviewing tourists, etc.). One strategy used by teachers in supporting and framing coursework was to hold a class discussion so that relevant arguments and theories could be shared, a tactic that could prove useful in a mixed ability group.

While the structuring of lower attaining students' work may extend their thinking it may, simultaneously, limit their independent learning by channelling them in particular directions which prevent them from exploring other avenues. That is, in some cases the teachers explicitly limit the parameters for creativity to maximise the 'average' opportunity for students to do well. However, by structuring coursework teachers may 'debar' lower attaining students from attaining their potential, but this might not be possible within the confines of (the particular) coursework, so the student's actual mark would be greater than that attained without structure (see 'Strategies for enhancing evaluation skills', pages 14-16). Teachers were not sure whether this ceiling of attainment was a reality. Students were seen as having autonomy in completing coursework with the flexibility and options available in the process.

Support and feedback

Teachers invested considerable time and energy in supporting students by way of feedback. However, specific messages of what students could do to improve their work were not realised. Students typically could not articulate what 'better' looked like (with reference to a particular piece of work) and could talk only in terms of 'better spelling and punctuation' or 'more of something'. The quality-quantity dimension is a further misperception that teachers cannot overemphasise. Indeed it would seem that teachers, unwittingly, confirm this myth that many students hold (see also Chapter 3).

One teacher recognised the importance to her own progress of knowing what was expected of her students, but she did not see an immediate parallel with the importance of students having this knowledge for themselves:

> **Teacher:** *I've certainly found over the years that one of the reasons why my classroom teaching has improved is because I know what's expected. I know what the exam board are looking for and know the way their minds work ... and it's so much easier to be able to guide the students to be able to do really good pieces of work.*

Support and scaffolding feature strongly in teachers' structuring of coursework and in helping students to maximise their attainment. Interestingly, the focus of support and scaffolding tends to be on attainment rather than on improving learning (see Leat and McGrane, 2000). Typically metacognitive strategies are associated with higher ability students, but it also seems to be key for students' awareness to be raised in regard to:

- what thinking skills are;
- how they are evidenced/can be demonstrated;
- how 'thinking about thinking' can enhance students' work.

While these are difficult to achieve explicitly for many students, and possibly only those who are 'within sight' of demonstrating such skills, it can be addressed implicitly. For example, through peer assessment or by assessing exemplars using assessment criteria, i.e. increasing the formative dimensions to students' experience of teaching and learning, as suggested in Chapter 3 (pages 19-23).

The analysis of their responses to writing coursework suggested that, according to their ability, students require quite different levels of feedback if the teacher is to enable a student to improve his or her learning. Developing students' critical faculties, and thus enhancing their skills as decision makers, is crucial. In other words, helping the students to make critical judgements about the validity (and hence quality) of their work requires similar attention to analytical thought and understanding of the processes of learning on the part of the teacher. And of course the student needs time to come to terms with the implications for developing reflective approaches to coursework. Clearly, there is a need and an opportunity to re-orientate feedback towards developing students' learning, for example in relation to thinking skills, and for this to be for all students and not simply those who are 'within sight' of demonstrating such skills. There is something to be said for helping students become aware of their thinking about thinking, whatever their current level of reasoning, rather than simply aim it at the higher ability students because that is the level at which it will be *explicitly* evidenced. Teachers thus have a key role in developing appropriate formative feedback.

Structuring coursework to maximise attainment

The utilisation of enabling strategies, frameworks and structuring was important to the teachers. Good teaching in coursework was seen as providing a supportive structure while, at the same time, allowing the students to make their own decisions regarding process and content. However, there was some agreement that coursework offers a greater challenge for lower attaining students and that the incorporation of coursework in the GCSE framework allowed that particular group to achieve better grades. The teachers thought that the degree of support that students need to help them make choices and maximise their marks, as opposed to being allowed the flexibility to develop their own ideas more fully, created a tension. The teachers wondered if students felt this tension. In the case of lower ability students there was a consensus that structuring was necessary to maximise marks attained.

Modelling as support

It was widely agreed that teachers could help students by modelling their expectations of doing coursework, by providing examples of good and poor coursework (i.e. meeting criteria and not meeting criteria) and by involving students in discussions about coursework. Although we found little evidence of modelling being used for coursework, it is seen by some teachers as a major tool for effective teaching.

> **Teacher 1:** *You have to model and an effective teacher does model and show. And they're constantly thinking on their feet and giving examples. Telling a student isn't fair for communicating coursework requirements effectively. What you need to do with students is show them examples of A and E grade work, then together you come to a consensus about what is a successful piece of coursework, so that that is about ownership.*
>
> **Teacher 2:** *Students ask 'Is this right?' 'Is this what it should look like?' and we've discussed this and ways in which we can support that and we're very keen at the moment on modelling things for students. Giving them a good example either from the work that's coming out of the class or one that's come from a different class or one we've written ourselves. We don't necessarily give it out to them and say 'Here it is', but I know one of the teachers will put it on an OHP and say 'This is a good example of an introduction. Let's have a look at it.'*

Summary

Case-by-case and school-by-school, there was a mismatch between teachers' strategies for communicating coursework requirements effectively and students' understanding of the requirements. In particular, teacher feedback did not consistently match the weaknesses identified in students' work. While teachers believe they are clear in terms of their expectations for completing coursework and communicating this to their students, in our experience 'telling students' or 'giving them a booklet' are simply not sufficient. Students would be better helped by teachers modelling their expectations of doing coursework, by the provision of examples of good and poor coursework, and, most importantly, by discussing both with students. In this way teachers and students can reap the benefits of formative assessment strategies that help improve both the process and the product of coursework (Black and Wiliam, 1998).

> ## Points to consider
> In relation to the fieldwork component of GCSE Geography coursework:
>
> - What role does modelling play in your support for student learning through coursework?
>
> - What other strategies might you use to develop the formative dimension to learning through coursework?

Photo: Liz Taylor

6: Conclusion and ways forward

We found that, through coursework, students often engage in a hybrid learning experience in which autonomy in the organisation of the individual learning process is mediated and constricted by teachers and their interpretations of a heavily prescribed coursework and assessment framework. However, there is considerable scope for working towards a greater element of subsuming the requirements of assessment of learning within a more formative assessment framework, i.e. assessment *for* learning. In particular, notions of students being encouraged to be more involved in their own learning and progress, specifically developing understanding between teachers and students about assessment criteria, conceptions of evaluation, targets and, perhaps most crucially, what 'better looks like'. These key areas can bring out the complementary qualities of assessment *of* learning and assessment *for* learning.

Overall, we suggest that teachers, parents and students value the skills of creativity, critical thinking and independent learning, and that coursework has an important role in giving students opportunities to develop and demonstrate them. In contrast to recent political thinking (e.g. the National Advisory Committee on Creative and Cultural Education report (DfEE, 1999)) the development and demonstration of creativity, critical thinking and independent learning does not require the abandonment of existing approaches to learning, or replacement by new ones. GCSE Geography coursework is typically viewed as an evolutionary rather than a revolutionary change to learning practices. Substantial change in the approaches to learning of students of all abilities does not occur, although the significance, value and intensification of current approaches are well recognised, particularly in the amount of time now spent on coursework.

While students recognise that coursework fosters creative exchanges of ideas and approaches to learning, these benefits are not transferred readily to other situations. On the one hand, the skills associated with creativity, critical thinking and independent learning are important in producing good quality coursework. On the other, our evidence indicates that such process skills are of secondary importance to the goal of achieving a good GCSE grade for coursework. Getting 'marks in the bank' (students), constraints from assessment criteria (teachers), and pressure from accountability, e.g. league tables (parents and teachers), all promote the importance of maximising students' grades. Such high-stakes factors increasingly influence the practice of completing coursework to the extent that the promotion of creativity, critical thinking and independent learning is second in order of importance. While the *status quo* is not likely to change in the short term, for teachers and other stakeholders, it would be appropriate to redress the balance so that greater attention is given to the process of coursework, both for itself and in enhancing the product.

Ways forward

There appears to be a shift in the way that teachers and students play the 'assessment game' at GCSE – now knowing the rules of the game, they are trying to 'box clever'. At the inception of GCSEs, coursework was perceived to enhance the validity of the assessment process. It is now also evident that creativity, critical thinking and independent learning have a role in producing good quality GCSE Geography coursework. Now that teachers have learned the 'rules' they are aiming to maximise students' attainment, yet, as a consequence, the coursework element of the GCSE can begin to lose its discriminatory function. The irony is that this does not detract from the esteem in which teachers, students and parents hold coursework. It fulfils the original aspirations of enhancing opportunities for student learning, and is deemed to be both authentic and fair in the assessment framework.

Future research might corroborate or elaborate issues relating to the conditions and constraints affecting the identification, development and demonstration of creativity, critical thinking and independent learning. Our team of researchers proposed three levels at which this might be approached in investigating student learning through coursework: the individual, the subject and the school levels.

At an individual level

Students
- What are the cognitive strengths and weaknesses displayed by the student?

- Does his/her personality and motivation conform to the traditional view of the creative, critical, and/or independent person? What role do social-psychological factors play?

- How does the student cope with controversy in his/her coursework, and how is this related to his/her perception of locus of control in learning?

- From a longitudinal perspective, how are creativity, critical thinking and independent learning related to different points in a learner's life history, and to coursework in different subject areas?

Teachers
- How can teachers be encouraged to move away from treating teaching towards examinations and teaching for lifelong learning as mutually exclusive?

- How can teachers be supported in developing strategies that support creativity, critical thinking and independent learning and student autonomy in geography coursework, and in effectively communicating strategies for best performance, i.e. enhancing the process without teachers feeling they are endangering the quality of the outcome?

At the subject level

- What effects does the nature of geography as a subject have on students' work?

- What kinds of creative, critical and independent practices are routinely engaged with in secondary school geography? On what grounds are they effective?

- In what ways is geography at key stages 3 and 4 a contribution to lifelong learning? How is it susceptible to the development of creativity, critical thinking and independent learning? And, of course, what are geography teachers' understandings and interpretations of the issues and challenges this raises?

- More concretely, how, for example, might the greater emphasis on information and communications technology in coursework in GCSE specifications enhance student learning in relation to creativity, critical thinking and independent learning? Or, to what extent can these elements be encouraged through all subjects?

At a school level

- What roles might middle and senior management play in encouraging and adopting approaches that raise the status of creativity, critical thinking and independent learning at student, teacher and department levels?

- To what extent are the conditions and constraints for developing creativity, critical thinking and independent learning socially and culturally located, within and outside the school?

There were clear messages about the valuable ways teachers supported their students and, in so doing, differentiated according to perceptions of need and ability – but we want to question the sufficiency of these and the 'assumed dimension' that students were not being disadvantaged by these approaches. Clearly there is scope for further research to be done in promoting and integrating formative assessment features into the classroom. Our hope is that this book has encouraged teachers to think what 'better' looks like for them in their classrooms and to play a part in raising the ceiling on students' attainment.

Bibliography

Bailin, S. (1999) 'Common misconceptions of critical thinking', *Journal of Curriculum Studies*, 31, 3, pp. 269-83.

Balderstone, D. and Lambert, D. (1999) 'Sunday evening at the kitchen table', *Teaching Geography*, 24, 2, pp. 89-91.

Barratt, R., Burgess, H. and Cass, D. (1997) 'An enquiry approach to geography fieldwork', *Teaching Geography*, 22, 2, pp. 77-81.

Black, P. and Wiliam, D. (1998) 'Assessment and classroom learning', *Assessment in Education*, 5, 1, pp. 7-74.

Bland, K., Chambers, B., Donert, K. and Thomas, T. (1996) 'Fieldwork' in Bailey, P. and Fox, P. (eds) *Geography Teachers' Handbook*. Sheffield: Geographical Association, pp. 165-75.

Brown, P. and Lauder, H. (1992) (eds) *Education for Economic Survival: From Fordism to post-Fordism?* London: Routledge.

Butt, G. (2000) 'The place of assessment in geographical education' in Fisher, C. and Binns, T. (eds) *Issues in Geography Teaching*. London: Routledge Falmer, pp. 234-44.

Cooper, P. and McIntyre, D. (1996) *Effective Teaching and Learning: Teachers' and students' perspectives*. Buckingham: Open University Press.

DfEE (Department for Education and Employment) (1998) *The Learning Age* (Green Paper). London: DfEE.

DfEE (1999) *All Our Futures*. London: DfEE.

DfEE/QCA (Qualifications and Curriculum Authority) (1999) *The National Curriculum: Handbook for secondary teachers in England (key stages 3 and 4)*. London: DfEE/QCA.

Erickson, F. and Shultz, J. (1992) 'Students' experience of the curriculum' in Jackson, P.W. (ed) *Handbook of Research on Curriculum*. New York: Macmillan, pp. 465-85.

Foskett, N. (2000) 'Fieldwork and the development of thinking skills', *Teaching Geography*, 25, 3, pp. 126-9.

Gipps, C. (1992) 'National curriculum assessment: a research agenda', *British Educational Research Journal*, 18, 3, pp. 277-86.

Howes, N. and Flinders, K. (1998) 'Assessing GCSE coursework', *Teaching Geography*, 23, 4, pp. 204-5.

Howes, N. and Hopkin, J. (2000) 'Improving formative assessment in geography', *Teaching Geography*, 25, 3, pp. 147-9.

Job, D., Day, C. and Smith, T. (1999) *Beyond the Bikesheds: Fresh approaches to fieldwork in the school locality*. Sheffield: Geographical Association.

Lambert, D. and Balderstone, D. (2000) *Learning to Teach Geography in the Secondary School*. London: Routledge Falmer.

Lambert, D. (2000) 'Using assessment to support learning' in Kent, A. (ed) *Reflective Practice in Geography Teaching*. London: Paul Chapman Publishing, pp. 131-40.

Leat, D. (ed) (1998) *Thinking Through Geography*. Cambridge: Chris Kington Publishing.

Leat, D. and McGrane, J. (2000) 'Diagnostic and formative assessment of students' thinking', *Teaching Geography*, 25, 1, pp. 4-7.

Macbeath, J. (1997) 'Unlock the secrets of the thinking brain', *Times Educational Supplement,* 20 June, p. 22.

Mackenzie, A. and White, R. (1982) 'Fieldwork in geography and long term memory structures', *American Educational Research Journal,* 19, 4, pp. 623-32.

McCallum, B., Hargreaves, E. and Gipps, C. (2000) 'Learning: the pupil's voice', *Cambridge Journal of Education*, 30, 2, pp. 275-89.

Morehouse, R. (1997) 'Critical thinking and the culture of the school', *Curriculum,* 18, 3, pp. 162-70.

Nowicki, M. (1999) 'Developing key skills through geography fieldwork', *Teaching Geography*, 24, 3, pp. 116-21.

OECD (Organisation for Economic Co-operation and Development) (1996) *Report on Korea*. Seoul: Korean Educational Development Institute.

Pollard, A., Thiessen, D. and Filer, A. (1997) *Children and their Curriculum: The perspectives of primary and elementary school children*. London: Falmer Press.

QCA (Qualifications and Curriculum Authority) (2001) *GCSE Criteria for Geography*. London: QCA.

Reid, A. and Jones, M. (2002) 'Learning from GCSE coursework', *Teaching Geography*, 27, 3, pp. 120-5.

Reynolds, D. (1997) 'East-west trade-off', *Times Educational Supplement*, 27 June, p. 21.

Rickinson, M. (2001) 'Learners and learning in environmental education: a critical review of the evidence', *Environmental Education Research*, 7, 3, pp. 208-320.

Ruddock, J., Chaplain, R. and Wallace, G. (eds) (1996) *School Improvement: What can students tell us?* London: David Fulton.

SEC (Secondary Examinations Council) (1985) *Working Paper 2: Coursework assessment in GCSE*. London: SEC.

Smith, P. (1997) 'Standards achieved: a review of geography in secondary schools in England, 1995-96', *Teaching Geography*, 22, 3, pp. 125-6.

Tattersall, K. (1994) 'The role and functions of public examinations', *Assessment in Education*, 1, pp. 293-305.